MASTERING FOREX TRADING

A COMPREHENSIVE GUIDE TO SUCCESS IN THE CURRENCY MARKETS

ABSOLUTEMPORIUM

CONTENTS

ABOUT THE AUTHOR

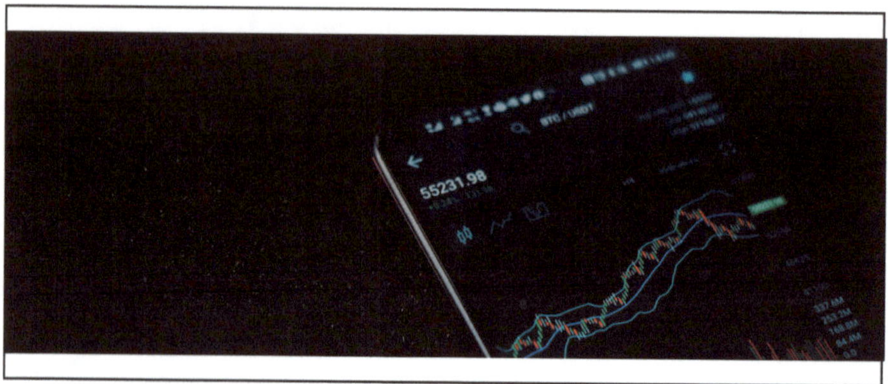

absolutemporium

Welcome to "Mastering Forex Trading: A Comprehensive Guide to Success in the Currency Markets" brought to you by Absolutemporium. We are excited to introduce you to the author behind this comprehensive guide, a seasoned trader with a passion for sharing knowledge and empowering beginners in the financial markets.

Our author is a respected expert in the field of trading, with years of experience navigating the dynamic world of forex and stocks. Starting as a curious novice, they embarked on their trading journey with determination, eager to understand the intricacies of the markets and develop winning strategies.

Throughout their trading career, the author encountered both triumphs and challenges, gaining invaluable insights that have shaped their unique approach to trading. Drawing from personal experiences, they understand the hurdles faced by beginners and the importance of a strong foundation for success.

Driven by a commitment to continuous learning, the author immersed themselves in the study of various trading methods, risk management techniques, and psychological discipline. Their thirst for knowledge led them to collaborate with industry experts, attend seminars, and engage with a diverse community of traders.

Through perseverance and dedication, the author achieved consistent profitability and financial independence, solidifying their status as a sought-after mentor and educator in the trading world. They have mentored numerous aspiring traders, guiding them on the path to becoming skilled and confident investors.

In this book, the author shares their extensive knowledge, practical tips, and proven strategies to equip beginners with the tools they need to succeed in the financial markets. Whether you are new to trading or seeking to refine your skills, the Trading Success Blueprint offers valuable insights that can help you achieve your trading goals.

As you embark on this journey with us, get ready to absorb the wisdom of our esteemed author, whose passion for trading and dedication to helping others will inspire and empower you to unlock your full potential in the exciting world of forex and stock trading.

Forex trading, the largest and most liquid financial market in the world, offers the potential for significant profits through the buying and selling of currencies. This chapter serves as your foundational step into the realm of forex trading, providing you with a comprehensive overview of the essential concepts and mechanics that drive this dynamic market.

CHAPTER I

At its core, forex trading involves the exchange of one currency for another, where traders aim to profit from fluctuations in currency values. The foreign exchange market operates 24 hours a day, five days a week, enabling participants from across the globe to engage in trading at any time.

Understanding Currency Pairs

Currencies are always traded in pairs. The first currency in the pair is the base currency, and the second is the quote currency. The exchange rate indicates how much of the quote currency is required to purchase one unit of the base currency. Major currency pairs, such as EUR/USD, USD/JPY, and GBP/USD, are the most commonly traded and provide high liquidity.

The Role of Major, Minor, and Exotic Pairs

Currency pairs can be categorized as major, minor, or exotic. Major pairs involve the world's strongest economies and currencies, and they typically have lower spreads due to their high trading volumes. Minor pairs include currencies from smaller economies, while exotic pairs combine a major currency with a currency from an emerging or less-established economy. Each category offers unique trading opportunities and risk profiles.

Factors Influencing Exchange Rates

Exchange rates are influenced by a variety of factors, including economic indicators, interest rates, political stability, and geopolitical events. Central banks play a significant role in influencing exchange rates through their monetary policies and interventions in the forex market.

Getting Acquainted with Leverage and Margin

Leverage allows traders to control a larger position size with a relatively small amount of capital. It magnifies both potential profits and losses. Margin, on the other hand, is the amount of money required to open and maintain a trading position. While leverage can enhance gains, it is crucial to exercise caution and implement proper risk management strategies.

Market Participants and Their Roles

Numerous participants contribute to the forex market's liquidity and volatility. Central banks, commercial banks, institutional investors, corporations, and individual traders all play distinct roles. Central banks, for instance, influence currency values through policy decisions, while commercial banks provide liquidity by facilitating transactions.

Why Engage in Forex Trading

Forex trading offers a range of opportunities for individuals seeking to participate in the financial markets. Some traders are attracted by the potential for high returns, while others appreciate the flexibility and accessibility of the market. Regardless of your motivations, developing a solid understanding of the market's mechanisms is essential before placing your first trade.

Technical The Importance of Education and Practice Analysis

Entering the forex market without proper knowledge and preparation is akin to sailing uncharted waters. Education is your compass, guiding you through the complexities of trading. Whether you're a beginner or an experienced trader, continuous learning is crucial to staying ahead in this ever-evolving landscape.

Navigating the Rest of the Guide

This guide is designed to equip you with the knowledge and tools necessary to navigate the forex market successfully. In the chapters that follow, you will delve deeper into technical and fundamental analysis, explore trading strategies, and learn about risk management and trading psychology. By mastering these aspects, you will be well on your way to becoming a confident and proficient forex trader.

As you embark on this journey, remember that forex trading is not a get-rich-quick scheme. It requires dedication, discipline, and a willingness to learn from both successes and setbacks. With the right mindset and a commitment to continuous improvement, you can harness the potential of the forex market to achieve your financial goals.

Choosing the Right Forex Broker

In the vast expanse of the forex market, the role of a forex broker is pivotal. A broker serves as your gateway to the world of currency trading, facilitating your access to the market, executing your trades, and providing essential tools and resources. However, with an overwhelming array of broker options available, each boasting various features and promises, the task of choosing the right broker can be a daunting one. This chapter aims to guide you through the process of evaluating and selecting a forex broker that aligns with your trading goals, risk tolerance, and trading style.

Understanding the Broker's Role: Your Trading Ally

Before delving into the specifics of choosing a broker, it's crucial to understand the role a broker plays in your trading journey. A broker is essentially an intermediary that connects you to the global forex market. They provide you with a trading platform — a software that allows you to view price charts, execute trades, and access various trading tools. Additionally, brokers offer leverage, enabling you to control larger positions with a smaller investment. Some brokers also offer educational resources, analysis tools, and customer support.

Regulation and Compliance: The Pillars of Trust

One of the fundamental aspects to consider when choosing a broker is their regulatory status. Regulation is essential as it ensures that the broker operates within a framework of rules and guidelines set by regulatory authorities. These regulations are designed to protect traders' interests, prevent fraud, and ensure a fair trading environment. Regulatory bodies, such as the Financial Conduct Authority (FCA) in the UK or the Commodity Futures Trading Commission (CFTC) in the US, oversee brokers' activities and ensure they adhere to stringent standards. When selecting a broker, prioritize those that are regulated by reputable authorities.

Broker Reputation and Reviews: Insights from Fellow Traders

Gauging a broker's reputation is an integral step in the decision-making process. Online reviews, forums, and discussions provide invaluable insights into the experiences of other traders with a particular broker. By examining both positive and negative reviews, you can gain a holistic understanding of the broker's strengths and weaknesses. However, exercise discernment when evaluating reviews, as not all experiences are representative of the broker's overall quality.

Trading Platforms and Tools: Your Trading Hub

The trading platform is your central hub for executing trades, analyzing markets, and accessing various trading tools. When evaluating a broker's trading platform, consider factors such as usability, features, and compatibility with your devices. Look for platforms that offer customizable charting tools, a variety of technical indicators, and real-time news updates. The platform should be intuitive and user-friendly, enabling you to navigate the complex world of forex trading with ease.

Spreads, Commissions, and Fees: The Cost of Trading

Every trade you execute involves costs, and understanding these costs is vital to managing your trading expenses effectively. Spreads — the difference between the bid and ask prices — are a primary source of revenue for brokers. Lower spreads can enhance your trading profitability, so compare spreads across different brokers to identify competitive rates. Additionally, some brokers charge commissions or fees per trade, which can impact your overall trading costs. When evaluating spreads and fees, consider the quality of the broker's services and tools in relation to the costs incurred.

Available Assets and Markets: Diversification Opportunities

While forex trading revolves around currency pairs, some brokers offer access to other financial instruments such as commodities, indices, and cryptocurrencies. If you're interested in diversifying your trading portfolio, consider brokers that provide a wide range of tradable assets. However, prioritize the quality and reliability of the broker's forex offerings before considering additional asset classes.

Leverage and Margin Requirements: Balancing Risk and Reward

Leverage is a double-edged sword in forex trading — it amplifies both potential profits and potential losses. When evaluating a broker's leverage options, consider your risk tolerance, trading strategy, and capital availability. High leverage can offer the potential for significant gains, but it also magnifies the risk of losses. Therefore, ensure that the broker's leverage offerings align with your risk management plan.

Customer Support: A Lifeline in Trading

In the dynamic world of forex trading, timely and effective customer support can make a significant difference. Evaluate the broker's customer support channels, such as phone, email, and live chat, and assess their response times. A reliable broker should offer prompt and helpful customer support, especially during market hours when quick assistance can be crucial to your trading decisions.

Educational Resources: Nurturing Your Trading Knowledge

A broker's commitment to your success is often reflected in the educational resources they offer. Look for brokers that provide educational materials such as webinars, tutorials, trading guides, and market analysis. These resources can enhance your trading knowledge, help you develop effective strategies, and empower you to make informed trading decisions.

Deposit and Withdrawal Methods: Seamless Fund Transfers

Smooth and secure fund transfers are essential to your trading experience. Evaluate the deposit and withdrawal methods offered by the broker, as well as the processing times and any associated fees. A broker that supports a variety of payment methods and ensures swift and hassle-free transactions contributes to a seamless trading process.

Navigating the Broker Selection Process

Choosing the right forex broker is a decision that carries substantial weight in your trading journey. As you navigate the complex landscape of broker options, it's essential to approach the selection process with diligence, patience, and a critical mindset. By understanding the broker's role, prioritizing regulation and compliance, considering factors like reputation, trading platforms, spreads, and fees, you're equipped to make an informed decision that aligns with your trading aspirations.

In the chapters that follow, we will delve deeper into the mechanics of forex trading, exploring fundamental and technical analysis, advanced trading strategies, risk management, and the psychology that underpins successful trading. Armed with the knowledge gained from this chapter, you're poised to step confidently into the world of forex trading, ready to seize opportunities, navigate challenges, and craft a trading journey that aligns with your goals and aspirations.

In the intricate world of forex trading, understanding the fundamental concepts that drive market dynamics is akin to deciphering the code that underlies price movements. This chapter serves as a compass, guiding you through the essential principles that shape the forex landscape and equipping you with the foundational knowledge required to navigate this intricate terrain.

CHAPTER II

Market Participants, Unveiling the Players

The forex market is a bustling arena where a diverse cast of characters engages in trading activities. From central banks to individual retail traders, each participant plays a distinct role in shaping market dynamics.

- Central Banks: At the heart of the forex market are central banks. These financial institutions wield considerable influence by controlling interest rates and implementing monetary policies. Central banks use forex interventions to stabilize their currencies and foster economic growth.

- Commercial Banks: Commercial banks are instrumental in facilitating forex transactions. They offer a platform for market participants to exchange currencies and provide liquidity to ensure smooth trading operations.

- Institutional Investors: Hedge funds, mutual funds, pension funds, and other large-scale investors engage in forex trading as part of their broader investment strategies. These institutional players bring significant capital to the market, impacting liquidity and influencing price movements.

- Corporations: MNC engage in forex trading to hedge against currency risk. For instance, a company conducting international business may use forex contracts to mitigate potential losses caused by adverse currency fluctuations.

- Retail Traders: Individual traders like you contribute to the forex market's vibrancy. Advances in technology and the widespread availability of trading platforms have democratized forex trading, allowing retail traders to participate with relatively modest capital.

The Influence of Supply and Demand

At the heart of all economic activity lies the principle of supply and demand. In the context of forex trading, this principle is equally relevant. When demand for a currency surpasses its supply, its value appreciates. Conversely, when supply outstrips demand, the currency's value depreciates. Understanding supply and demand dynamics is pivotal for predicting price trends.

Understanding Forex Quotes and Pips

Forex quotes provide a snapshot of currency pair prices, offering insights into market conditions. A quote typically includes a bid price (the highest price buyers are willing to pay) and an ask price (the lowest price sellers are willing to accept). The difference between these prices is known as the spread. Pips, or percentage in point, represent the smallest price movement in a currency pair.

Interpreting Bid-Ask Spreads

The bid-ask spread reflects the cost of entering a trade. It is important to note that spreads can vary based on currency pairs, market conditions, and the broker you choose. Lower spreads are typically associated with major currency pairs due to their high liquidity, while exotic pairs tend to have wider spreads.

Leverage and Margin

Leverage is a double-edged sword in forex trading. It allows traders to control larger positions with a fraction of the capital required for a full trade. While leverage can amplify potential profits, it also magnifies potential losses. Proper risk management and understanding leverage ratios are crucial for preserving your trading capital.

The Impact of Economic Indicators

Economic indicators are vital instruments that provide insights into a country's economic health. These indicators, released at regular intervals, offer snapshots of key metrics such as Gross Domestic Product (GDP), unemployment rates, and inflation levels. Traders analyze economic indicators to anticipate potential shifts in currency values.

Central Banks and Interest Rates

Central banks hold a prominent place in the forex market due to their ability to influence currency values through interest rate decisions. Higher interest rates tend to attract foreign capital, leading to currency appreciation. Conversely, lower interest rates can result in currency depreciation as capital flows out of the country.

Political Stability and Geopolitical Events

Political stability and geopolitical events wield considerable influence over currency values. Political uncertainty can lead to currency fluctuations as investors and traders seek safe havens. Geopolitical events, such as trade agreements and conflicts, can trigger market volatility and impact exchange rates.

Charting Your Path Forward

The fundamental concepts explored in this chapter are the cornerstones of forex trading. By delving into the roles of different market participants, understanding supply and demand dynamics, interpreting forex quotes, and grasping the impact of economic indicators, you've equipped yourself with a solid foundation.

In the upcoming chapters, we will dive deeper into the intricacies of technical and fundamental analysis, exploring how these tools can be harnessed to make informed trading decisions. With each concept you grasp, you're one step closer to mastering the art of forex trading and navigating the challenges and opportunities that lie ahead.

Stay curious and engaged, for the journey ahead is both exciting and rewarding. As we delve deeper into the world of analysis and strategies, remember that a comprehensive understanding of these fundamental concepts will serve as your compass, guiding you through the complex currents of the forex market.

Limit your size in any position so that fear does not become the prevailing instinct guiding your judgment.

JOE VIDICH

As you embark on your forex trading journey, creating the right trading environment is akin to preparing the canvas for a masterpiece. This chapter serves as your guide to assembling the essential components that lay the foundation for successful trading. From selecting a reliable broker to practicing with demo accounts, each step contributes to shaping an environment conducive to informed decision-making and profitable outcomes.

CHAPTER III

Selecting a Reliable Forex Broker

Choosing a reputable and trustworthy forex broker is paramount to your trading success. A broker acts as an intermediary, providing you with access to the forex market and essential trading tools. When evaluating potential brokers, consider the following factors:

- Regulation: Opt for brokers regulated by respected authorities such as the U.S. Commodity Futures Trading Commission (CFTC), the U.K. Financial Conduct Authority (FCA), or the Australian Securities and Investments Commission (ASIC). Regulation ensures that brokers adhere to industry standards and practices.

- Available Currency Pairs: Ensure that the broker offers a variety of currency pairs, including major, minor, and exotic pairs. A diverse selection allows you to capitalize on a broader range of trading opportunities.

- Trading Platforms: The trading platform is your portal to the forex market. Look for brokers that offer user-friendly platforms with robust features. MetaTrader 4 (MT4) and MetaTrader 5 (MT5) are popular choices, known for their intuitive interfaces, advanced charting tools, and customizable indicators.

- Spreads and Commissions: Compare spreads across different brokers. Lower spreads can translate to reduced trading costs. Some brokers charge commissions per trade, so factor this into your decision-making process.

- Customer Support: Responsive and effective customer support is crucial. Test the broker's customer service through inquiries or demonstrations before committing.

Trading Platforms and Tools

A trading platform is your command center, providing you with the tools and resources necessary for analysis and execution. MetaTrader platforms, such as MT4 and MT5, offer a suite of features designed to enhance your trading experience:

- Advanced Charting Tools: Visualizing price movements is essential for effective analysis. Charts on trading platforms allow you to apply technical indicators, draw trendlines, and spot patterns that aid in decision-making.

- Technical Indicators and Oscillators: Indicators like Moving Averages, Relative Strength Index (RSI), and MACD offer insights into market trends, momentum, and potential reversals. Experiment with different indicators to develop your trading strategies.

- Automated Trading: Expert Advisors (EAs) are algorithms that automate trading processes based on predefined rules. EAs execute trades, manage positions, and even perform risk management tasks, freeing you from constant monitoring.

Demo Trading

Before committing real capital, immerse yourself in the world of trading through demo accounts. Demo accounts simulate real market conditions, enabling you to practice trading strategies and familiarize yourself with the trading platform without risking your money.

The Benefits of Demo Trading:

- Risk-Free Learning: Demo accounts provide a safe space to experiment with different trading strategies, hone your skills, and build confidence.

- Platform Familiarization:
  - Practice using the trading platform's features, such as placing orders, setting stop-loss and take-profit levels, and executing trades.

- Market Observation:
  - Analyze price movements, monitor charts, and test your ability to recognize patterns and trends.

- Refining Your Strategy:
  - Use demo trading to refine your trading plan, adjust risk management techniques, and develop a deeper understanding of market dynamics.

Getting Started with a Demo Account

- Select a Broker:
  - Choose a broker that offers a demo account alongside its live trading options.

- Download the Platform:
  - Download and install the broker's trading platform of your choice. Most brokers offer MetaTrader 4 (MT4) or MetaTrader 5 (MT5).

- Register for a Demo Account:
  - Sign up for a demo account using accurate personal information.

- Virtual Capital:
  - The demo account will be funded with virtual capital. This capital simulates trading conditions and allows you to practice without financial risk.

- Start Trading:
  - Begin experimenting with different trading strategies, analyzing charts, and placing simulated trades.

Utilizing Your Trading Environment

A well-crafted trading environment sets the stage for your forex trading journey. By selecting a reliable broker, familiarizing yourself with trading platforms and tools, and practicing with demo accounts, you're equipping yourself with the skills and knowledge needed to navigate the markets effectively.

In the following chapters, we will delve deeper into the analytical techniques that empower you to make informed trading decisions. As you progress, remember that building a strong foundation is key to achieving consistent success in the dynamic world of forex trading.

In the ever-shifting landscape of forex trading, the ability to decipher patterns, trends, and market dynamics is an invaluable skill. Technical analysis, often referred to as the art of reading price charts, equips traders with the tools to make informed decisions based on historical price data. This chapter delves into the world of technical analysis, unveiling its core principles and providing you with the knowledge to harness its power in your trading journey.

CHAPTER IV

The Language of Price

Technical analysis operates on the belief that market price movements reflect all available information. By analyzing historical price data, traders aim to predict future price movements and identify potential trade opportunities. This approach is grounded in the idea that history often repeats itself in the form of recognizable patterns.

Key Tenets of Technical Analysis:

- Price Discounts Everything: Technical analysis assumes that all information, whether economic, political, or psychological, is already reflected in price charts. Therefore, studying price patterns and trends provides insights into the collective market sentiment.

- Price Moves in Trends: The market tends to move in trends, characterized by sequences of higher highs and higher lows (uptrend) or lower highs and lower lows (downtrend). Recognizing trends is essential for making strategic trading decisions.

- History Tends to Repeat: Chart patterns and price movements tend to repeat over time due to human behavior and market psychology. This repetition forms the basis for identifying potential trade setups.

Candlestick Patterns:
Reading Price Action

Candlestick patterns are a visual representation of price movements over a specific time period, typically a day. Each candlestick conveys information about the opening, closing, high, and low prices during that period. Candlestick patterns offer insights into market sentiment and potential trend reversals.

- Bullish Candlesticks: A bullish (green or white) candlestick indicates that the closing price is higher than the opening price. Common patterns include the Hammer, Bullish Engulfing, and Morning Star, which signal potential price reversals.

- Bearish Candlesticks: A bearish (red or black) candlestick signifies that the closing price is lower than the opening price. Patterns like the Shooting Star, Bearish Engulfing, and Evening Star suggest potential downtrends.

Trendlines, Channels, and
Support/Resistance
Mapping Market Movements

- Channels: Channels encompass two parallel trendlines, forming a trading range. An ascending channel consists of an uptrend with parallel lines, while a descending channel represents a downtrend. Channels aid in identifying potential breakout or reversal points.

- Support and Resistance: Support levels are price points where a currency pair tends to stop falling and may bounce back, while resistance levels are where prices typically stall before declining. These levels are essential for setting stop-loss and take-profit orders.

Using Technical Indicators

Technical indicators are mathematical calculations based on historical price data, volume, or open interest. They provide quantitative insights into market trends, momentum, and potential reversals. Here are a few essential technical indicators:

- Moving Averages (MA): MAs smooth out price data by calculating the average over a specific period. They help identify trends and potential entry points. The 50-day and 200-day MAs are commonly used to assess long-term trends.

- Relative Strength Index (RSI): RSI measures the speed and change of price movements, indicating whether a currency pair is overbought (above 70) or oversold (below 30). It assists in spotting potential trend reversals.

- Moving Average Convergence Divergence (MACD): The MACD consists of two moving averages — the MACD line and the signal line. Crossovers and divergences between these lines provide insights into trend strength and potential shifts.

- Bollinger Bands: Bollinger Bands consist of a moving average and two standard deviation bands. They help identify periods of high volatility and potential price reversals.

The Power of Patterns

Chart patterns are formations on price charts that signal potential trend reversals or continuations. Recognizing these patterns enables traders to anticipate market movements and make informed decisions:

- Head and Shoulders Pattern: This reversal pattern includes a peak (head) between two lower peaks (shoulders). It indicates a potential trend reversal from bullish to bearish.

- Double Top and Double Bottom: Double Top forms after a strong uptrend, signaling a potential reversal. Double Bottom appears after a downtrend, suggesting a potential bullish reversal.

- Triangles (Ascending, Descending, Symmetrical): Triangles indicate a period of consolidation before a potential breakout. Ascending triangles suggest a bullish breakout, descending triangles imply a bearish breakout, and symmetrical triangles signal potential continuation or reversal.

Chart Patterns for Reversals and Continuations:

- Flags and Pennants: Flags and pennants are short-term continuation patterns that indicate a brief consolidation before the prevailing trend resumes. A flag is rectangular, while a pennant is triangular.

- Wedges (Rising and Falling): Wedges are similar to triangles but slope in the opposite direction. Rising wedges suggest potential bearish reversals, while falling wedges may signal bullish reversals.

Chart Patterns

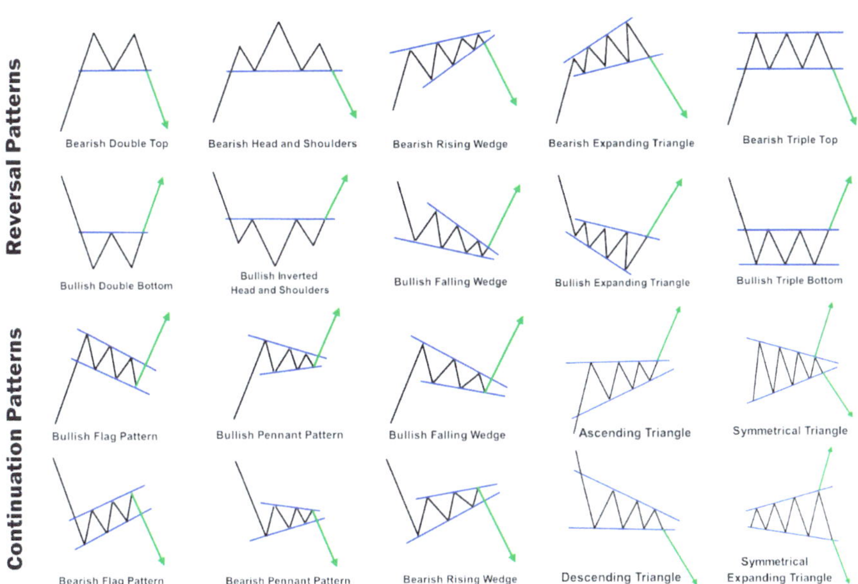

Technical analysis offers a plethora of tools and insights, but the key is integration. Combine different indicators, patterns, and tools to develop a holistic trading strategy that aligns with your risk tolerance, time commitment, and trading style.

Technical analysis is a skill that improves with practice. Engage in deliberate practice by analyzing historical charts, identifying patterns, and experimenting with different indicators. Over time, your ability to interpret price movements and make informed trading decisions will sharpen.

In the upcoming chapters, we will explore fundamental analysis, risk management, trading psychology, and advanced strategies, providing you with a comprehensive toolkit to navigate the complexities of the forex market.

The hard work in trading comes in the preparation. The actual process of trading, however, should be effortless.

JACK SCHWAGER

As you journey deeper into the realm of forex trading, an understanding of fundamental analysis becomes crucial. While technical analysis focuses on price patterns and historical data, fundamental analysis examines the underlying economic and geopolitical factors that influence currency movements. This chapter unveils the world of fundamental analysis, equipping you with the tools to decipher economic indicators, central bank policies, and global events that shape the forex market.

CHAPTER V

Understanding Fundamental Analysis: Peering Beyond the Charts

Fundamental analysis delves into the broader economic context that drives currency values. It explores the interplay between economic data, monetary policies, political stability, and geopolitical events, all of which contribute to the complex tapestry of the forex market.

Economic Indicators

Economic indicators are statistical measures that provide insights into a country's economic health. These indicators encompass a wide range of data, including GDP (Gross Domestic Product), inflation rates, unemployment figures, consumer spending, and trade balances. By analyzing these indicators, traders can gauge the overall state of an economy and anticipate potential shifts in currency values.

Key Economic Indicators:

- Gross Domestic Product (GDP):
GDP measures the total value of goods and services produced within a country's borders. A growing GDP is generally associated with a strong currency, reflecting economic vitality.

- Consumer Price Index (CPI):
CPI measures the average change in prices paid by consumers for a basket of goods and services. Rising CPI indicates inflation, which can erode purchasing power and weaken a currency.

- Unemployment Rate:
The unemployment rate reflects the percentage of the workforce that is unemployed and actively seeking employment. Lower unemployment rates are generally favorable for currency strength.

- Interest Rates and Monetary Policy:
Central banks influence currency values through changes in interest rates and monetary policy. Higher interest rates attract foreign investment, leading to currency appreciation, while lower rates can result in depreciation.

Central Bank Decisions

Central banks are pivotal players in the forex market. Their decisions on interest rates, money supply, and economic stimulus programs can have profound effects on currency values. Monitoring central bank announcements and understanding the rationale behind their policy decisions is essential for fundamental analysis.

Interest Rate Decisions: Central banks set interest rates as a means of controlling inflation and promoting economic growth. Higher interest rates tend to attract foreign capital seeking better returns, leading to currency appreciation.

Monetary Policy and Quantitative Easing

Central banks may engage in quantitative easing (QE) to stimulate economic activity. QE involves purchasing financial assets to inject liquidity into the economy. This can lead to currency depreciation due to increased money supply.

Economic Data Releases: Navigating the Calendar

Economic data releases, typically scheduled at specific times, offer insights into a country's economic performance. Traders closely monitor economic calendars to anticipate market movements and volatility that may accompany these releases.

Navigating Fundamentals and Technical

While fundamental and technical analyses are distinct approaches, they often complement each other. The confluence of strong fundamental data and confirming technical signals can provide traders with heightened confidence in their trading decisions.

Economic Events and Geopolitical Developments

Geopolitical events, such as elections, trade agreements, and conflicts, can significantly influence currency values. Political stability and international relations play a crucial role in shaping market sentiment and currency movements.

Risk Aversion and Safe-Haven Currencies: In times of geopolitical uncertainty or economic instability, investors may seek safety by flocking to safe-haven currencies like the US Dollar (USD), Japanese Yen (JPY), or Swiss Franc (CHF).

Global Economic Interdependence

In an interconnected world, the forex market is influenced by events beyond national borders. Developments in major economies can impact currencies across the globe.

Putting Fundamental Analysis into Practice

- Stay Informed: Stay updated on economic calendars, central bank announcements, and geopolitical developments that may impact currency values.

- Analyze Data Releases: Interpret economic indicators and assess their potential impact on currency movements.

- Assess Central Bank Policies: Understand the monetary policies and interest rate decisions of major central banks.

- Consider Geopolitical Events: Monitor international events that could trigger market volatility and affect currency values.

The Fusion of Analysis

By blending these two analytical approaches, you can develop a deeper understanding of market trends, anticipate potential reversals, and make informed trading decisions.

In the chapters ahead, we will explore the art of risk management, delve into the psychology of trading, and unveil advanced trading strategies that allow you to navigate the forex market with confidence and precision.

In the intricate dance of forex trading, success isn't simply a product of luck; it's the result of a well-crafted trading strategy and meticulous risk management. This chapter dives into the heart of trading, guiding you through the process of developing a robust trading strategy and implementing effective risk management techniques to safeguard your capital.

CHAPTER VI

Crafting Your Trading Strategy: Your Blueprint for Success

A trading strategy is your roadmap through the forex market. It encompasses a set of rules and guidelines that dictate your entry and exit points, position sizing, and overall approach to trading. A well-defined strategy provides structure, consistency, and a systematic approach to navigating the complexities of the market.

Identifying Your Trading Style

- **Scalping**: Scalpers aim to profit from short-term price movements by executing numerous trades within a day. This style requires quick decision-making and precise execution, which normally takes place in smaller timeframes (M1, M5,M30)

- **Day Trading**: Day traders open and close positions within the same trading day, avoiding overnight risk. They capitalize on intraday price fluctuations.

- **Swing Trading**: Swing traders hold positions for several days to weeks, aiming to capture larger price movements and trends.

- **Position Trading**: Position traders take a long-term perspective, holding positions for weeks to months. They base their decisions on fundamental analysis and broader market trends.

Components of Your Trading Strategy

- **Entry and Exit Rules:** Define clear criteria for entering and exiting trades. This may involve technical indicators, chart patterns, or a combination of both.

- **Risk-Reward Ratio**: Determine your desired risk-reward ratio for each trade. A common ratio is 1:2, meaning you aim to make twice the potential profit compared to your potential loss.

- **Position Sizing:** Calculate the size of each trade based on your risk tolerance and the distance between your entry and stop-loss levels.

- **Timeframes:** Choose the timeframe that aligns with your trading style. Short-term traders may focus on lower timeframes, while long-term traders analyze higher timeframes.

- **Trading Plan:** Document your strategy in a comprehensive trading plan that outlines your goals, rules, and risk management procedures.

Risk Management
Safeguarding Your Capital

Effective risk management is the cornerstone of sustainable trading. It ensures that no single trade can wipe out a substantial portion of your capital and allows you to withstand the inevitable ups and downs of the market.

Determining Your Risk Tolerance

- **Risk Percentage**

Decide what percentage of your trading capital you're willing to risk on each trade. A common guideline is to risk no more than 1-2% of your capital on a single trade.

- **Risk per Trade**

Calculate the dollar amount you're comfortable risking on each trade based on your risk percentage and capital.

Setting Stop-Loss and Take-Profit Levels

- **Stop-Loss**

Place a stop-loss order at a level that, if reached, would signal that your trade thesis is invalidated. This limits potential losses.

- **Take-Profit:**

Determine a take-profit level that aligns with your risk-reward ratio and the potential price movement of the currency pair.

Diversification and Correlation
The Art of Spreading Risk

- **Currency Diversification**

Avoid concentrating your trades on a single currency pair. Diversification spreads risk and reduces the impact of a single trade's outcome on your overall capital.

- **Correlation Analysis**

Consider the correlation between currency pairs. Positive correlation means pairs move in the same direction, while negative correlation means they move in opposite directions.

Emotions and Discipline - The Psychology of Trading

Trading psychology plays a significant role in your success. Emotions like fear, greed, and impatience can cloud your judgment and lead to poor decision-making. Develop a disciplined mindset by:

- **Sticking to Your Plan**: Execute trades according to your strategy, even if emotions tempt you to deviate.
- **Managing Expectations**: Understand that losses are part of trading. Focus on long-term profitability rather than short-term wins.
- **Avoiding Overtrading**: Overtrading can deplete your capital and lead to emotional burnout. Stick to your predefined trades.

Backtesting and Continuous Improvement:

- **Backtesting**: Test your trading strategy using historical data to assess its performance and identify areas for improvement.
- **Adapt and Adjust**: Markets evolve, and your strategy should too. Continuously assess your strategy and make adjustments as needed.

The Synergy of Strategy and Risk Management

The synergy between a well-defined trading strategy and effective risk management is the key to enduring success in forex trading. By adhering to your strategy, managing risk, and cultivating discipline, you position yourself for consistent profitability and the ability to navigate the market's twists and turns.

In the upcoming chapters, we will delve into advanced trading strategies, explore the nuances of trading psychology, and provide you with the tools to optimize your trading performance.

As you start learning about forex trading, it's really important to understand how to read chart patterns and use technical indicators. Chart patterns show how people feel about the market, and indicators help analyze how prices are changing. In this part, we will teach you how to study charts and use indicators. This will help you find good chances to trade and make smart decisions.

CHAPTER VII

Chart Patterns - Deciphering Market Sentiment

Chart patterns are visual representations of market movements and psychology. These patterns emerge as traders respond to shifts in supply and demand dynamics, forming shapes that signal potential trend continuations or reversals.

Common Chart Patterns

- **Head and Shoulders**

This pattern consists of three peaks — an initial peak (head) flanked by two smaller peaks (shoulders). A neckline connects the lows between the shoulders. A head and shoulders pattern signals a potential trend reversal from bullish to bearish or vice versa.

- **Double Top and Double Bottom**

A double top forms after a sustained uptrend and indicates a potential bearish reversal. Conversely, a double bottom forms after a downtrend and signals a potential bullish reversal.

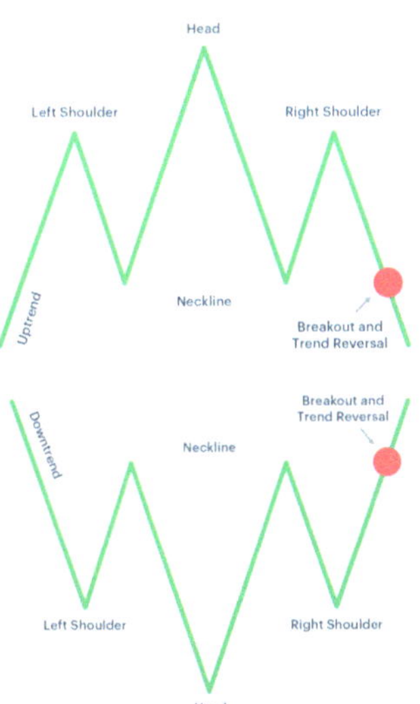

- **Triangles (Ascending, Descending, Symmetrical)**

Triangles reflect a period of consolidation before a potential breakout. An ascending triangle suggests a bullish breakout, a descending triangle indicates a bearish breakout, and a symmetrical triangle suggests potential continuation or reversal.

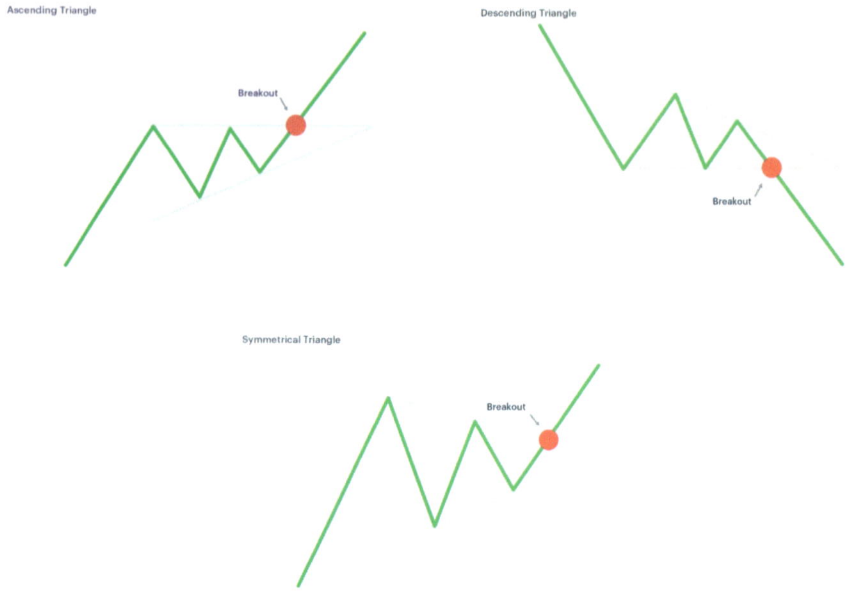

- **Flags and Pennants**

Flags and pennants are short-term continuation patterns that develop after a strong price movement. A flag is a rectangular pattern, while a pennant is triangular. These patterns suggest a brief consolidation before the prevailing trend resumes.

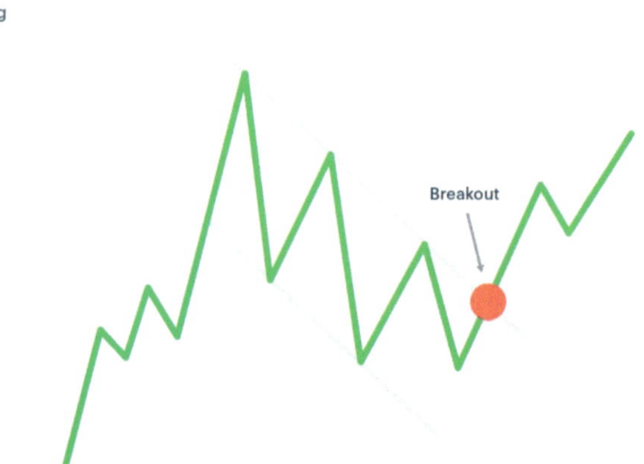

Technical Indicators - Insights from Data and Math

Technical indicators are mathematical calculations based on historical price data and volume. These tools offer quantitative insights into market trends, momentum, and potential reversals, aiding traders in making informed decisions.

- **Oscillators: Momentum and Overbought/Oversold Conditions**

Relative Strength Index (RSI): The RSI measures the speed and change of price movements. It oscillates between 0 and 100, with values above 70 indicating overbought conditions and values below 30 indicating oversold conditions.

- **Stochastic Oscillator**

The stochastic oscillator compares the closing price to its price range over a certain period. Values above 80 suggest overbought conditions, while values below 20 suggest oversold conditions.

Trend Following Indicators - Capturing Price Movements

- **Moving Averages (MA)**

Moving averages smooth out price data, revealing the underlying trend. The crossover of short-term (faster) and long-term (slower) moving averages may signal potential trend reversals.

- **Moving Average Convergence Divergence (MACD)**

The MACD consists of two moving averages — the MACD line and the signal line. Crossovers and divergences between these lines offer insights into trend strength and potential shifts.

Volatility Indicators - Gauging Market Fluctuations

- **Bollinger Bands**

Bollinger Bands consist of a moving average and two standard deviation bands. Expanding bands indicate increased volatility, while contracting bands suggest reduced volatility. Price often returns to the middle band (moving average).

- **Average True Range (ATR)**

ATR measures market volatility by calculating the average range between high and low prices over a specified period.

Putting Patterns and Indicators into Action - A Holistic Approach

- **Pattern Confirmation**

When a chart pattern forms, wait for a confirmation before executing a trade. This could involve a breakout, a reversal candlestick pattern, or convergence with indicators.

- **Confluence of Indicators**

Consider the confluence of signals from different indicators. When multiple indicators align, they can provide stronger confirmation for potential trades.

- **Avoiding Pitfalls - The Importance of Context**

While chart patterns and indicators offer valuable insights, they are not foolproof. Market context, news events, and fundamental factors can influence price movements. Always consider the bigger picture and exercise caution when relying solely on technical analysis.

Continuous Learning and Adaptation - The Path to Mastery

As you navigate the intricate landscape of chart patterns and indicators, remember that mastery is an ongoing journey. Practice, analysis, and continuous learning will enhance your ability to interpret patterns, interpret indicators, and make effective trading decisions.

Your Chart Patterns and Indicators Arsenal

Chart patterns and technical indicators are powerful tools in a trader's toolkit. By honing your ability to identify and interpret chart patterns and indicators, you can elevate your trading strategy to new heights. Remember, success lies in the delicate balance between artful pattern recognition and the precision of data-driven indicators.

In the chapters ahead, we will delve deeper into advanced trading techniques, explore the psychology of trading, and equip you with the skills to adapt and thrive in the ever-evolving forex market.

Entering trades and managing positions are crucial aspects of forex trading that can significantly impact your trading success. In this chapter, we will explore various order types for entering and exiting trades, the importance of setting stop-loss orders to manage risk, effective techniques for monitoring and managing open positions, and strategies for scaling in and out of trades. Additionally, we will delve into the art of responding to news and events, which can have a profound impact on the forex market.

CHAPTER VIII

Entering Trades: The Art of Precision Execution

When it comes to entering trades, precision is key. Traders must be able to execute their trades swiftly and accurately to capture favorable market movements. There are several order types available to enter trades, each serving specific purposes.

1. Market Orders

A market order is the most straightforward type of order, where traders buy or sell a currency pair at the current market price. This type of order is suitable when speed is essential, and traders want to enter the trade immediately. Market orders are executed at the prevailing market price, which means there may be slight price variations due to market volatility and liquidity.

2. Limit Orders

A limit order is an order to buy or sell a currency pair at a specific price or better. Traders use limit orders when they believe that the market will reach a particular price level before moving in their favor. For example, if the current price of EUR/USD is 1.1800, and a trader believes that the price will dip to 1.1750 before rising, they can place a buy limit order at 1.1750. If the market reaches that price, the order will be executed, and the trader will enter the trade.

3. Stop Orders

Stop orders are orders that are triggered when the market reaches a specific price level. There are two types of stop orders:

Buy Stop: A buy stop order is placed above the current market price, and it is triggered when the price reaches or goes above the specified level. Traders use buy stop orders when they expect the price to break out of a resistance level and continue rising.

Sell Stop: A sell stop order is placed below the current market price, and it is triggered when the price reaches or goes below the specified level. Traders use sell stop orders when they expect the price to break down from a support level and continue falling.

Using these order types effectively requires a thorough understanding of technical and fundamental analysis, as well as the ability to make swift and accurate decisions.

Exiting Trades: Take-Profit Orders and Trailing Stops

Equally important to entering trades is knowing when and how to exit them. Properly executed exits can lock in profits and protect against potential losses. Two common methods for exiting trades are take-profit orders and trailing stops.

1. Take-Profit Orders

A take-profit order is an instruction to close a trade once a specified profit target is reached. By setting a take-profit level, traders ensure that profitable trades are automatically closed, preventing the market from reversing and eroding gains.

To set a take-profit level, traders should consider their risk-reward ratio and the potential price movement of the currency pair. For example, if a trader risks 50 pips to potentially gain 100 pips, they may set a take-profit level at 100 pips above their entry price.

2. Trailing Stops:

A trailing stop is a dynamic stop-loss order that adjusts as the trade moves in the trader's favor. It allows traders to lock in profits while also giving the trade room to breathe and potentially capture additional gains.

With a trailing stop, the stop-loss level moves automatically with the price in the direction of the trade. If the market moves in favor of the trader, the stop-loss level will trail behind the price at a specified distance. However, if the market reverses and moves against the trader, the stop-loss level remains fixed, protecting against excessive losses.

Trailing stops are particularly useful in trending markets, as they allow traders to ride the trend while protecting their profits.

- **Setting Stop-Loss Orders: Managing Risk and Protecting Capital**

Setting stop-loss orders is a fundamental aspect of risk management in forex trading. A stop-loss order is an instruction to close a trade when the market reaches a specified price level, preventing further losses beyond a predetermined point.

- **The Importance of Stop-Loss Orders**

Stop-loss orders are critical for managing risk and protecting trading capital. By setting a stop-loss level, traders define the maximum amount they are willing to risk on a trade. This helps prevent large and potentially catastrophic losses that can significantly impact a trading account.

Strategies for Setting Stop-Loss Orders

Technical Levels: Place stop-loss orders beyond key technical support or resistance levels to minimize the likelihood of the market hitting the stop-loss prematurely.

Volatility Considerations: Adjust stop-loss levels based on market volatility. In highly volatile conditions, widen the stop-loss to avoid premature exits.

Trailing Stops: As discussed earlier, trailing stops can be used to adjust the stop-loss level as the trade moves in the trader's favor, locking in profits and reducing risk.

Remember that the stop-loss level should be determined based on the trader's risk tolerance, trading strategy, and the specific market conditions.

Monitoring and Managing Open Positions:

Once a trade is executed, effective monitoring and management of open positions are vital for optimizing trading performance.

Regular Monitoring: Keep a close eye on open positions, assessing their progress relative to your trading plan and strategy.

Avoid Over-monitoring: While monitoring is essential, over-analyzing positions can lead to impulsive decisions based on short-term market fluctuations. Trust your analysis and stick to your plan.

Trade Journal: Maintain a trade journal to record trade details, emotions, and outcomes. A trade journal helps you track your trading decisions and learn from successes and mistakes.

Scaling In and Out of Positions:

Scaling in and out of positions involves gradually increasing or decreasing the position size as the trade progresses. This technique can be employed in various ways, depending on the trader's strategy and market conditions.

Scaling In: Gradually add to a winning position as the trade moves in your favor. This approach allows you to capitalize on momentum while managing risk.

Scaling Out: Scale out of a position by partially closing the trade as it moves in your favor. This strategy locks in profits while still keeping exposure to potential further gains.

Scaling in and out requires careful consideration and risk management, as it affects the overall position size and risk exposure.

Strategies for Setting Stop-Loss Orders

Technical Levels: Place stop-loss orders beyond key technical support or resistance levels to minimize the likelihood of the market hitting the stop-loss prematurely.

Volatility Considerations: Adjust stop-loss levels based on market volatility. In highly volatile conditions, widen the stop-loss to avoid premature exits.

Trailing Stops: As discussed earlier, trailing stops can be used to adjust the stop-loss level as the trade moves in the trader's favor, locking in profits and reducing risk.

Remember that the stop-loss level should be determined based on the trader's risk tolerance, trading strategy, and the specific market conditions.

Monitoring and Managing Open Positions:

Once a trade is executed, effective monitoring and management of open positions are vital for optimizing trading performance.

Regular Monitoring: Keep a close eye on open positions, assessing their progress relative to your trading plan and strategy.

Avoid Over-monitoring: While monitoring is essential, over-analyzing positions can lead to impulsive decisions based on short-term market fluctuations. Trust your analysis and stick to your plan.

Trade Journal: Maintain a trade journal to record trade details, emotions, and outcomes. A trade journal helps you track your trading decisions and learn from successes and mistakes.

Scaling In and Out of Positions:

Scaling in and out of positions involves gradually increasing or decreasing the position size as the trade progresses. This technique can be employed in various ways, depending on the trader's strategy and market conditions.

Scaling In: Gradually add to a winning position as the trade moves in your favor. This approach allows you to capitalize on momentum while managing risk.

Scaling Out: Scale out of a position by partially closing the trade as it moves in your favor. This strategy locks in profits while still keeping exposure to potential further gains.

Scaling in and out requires careful consideration and risk management, as it affects the overall position size and risk exposure.

If most traders would
learn to sit on their hands
50 percent of the time,
they would make a lot
more money.

BILL LIPSCHUTZ

In the dynamic world of forex trading, the art of risk management and money management is the compass that guides you through the turbulent waters of uncertainty. It's the shield that safeguards your capital and ensures your longevity as a trader. This chapter delves into the intricate interplay between risk management and money management, unveiling strategies that empower you to preserve your capital, manage losses, and optimize your trading performance.

CHAPTER IX

Risk Management - The Pillar of Trading Success

Risk management is the bedrock upon which successful trading is built. It's the practice of identifying potential risks and taking proactive measures to mitigate their impact. By mastering risk management, you can navigate the market's ebbs and flows while maintaining financial stability.

Determining Your Risk Tolerance - The Golden Rule

Risk Percentage: Determine the percentage of your trading capital you're willing to risk on a single trade. A common guideline is to risk no more than 1-2% of your capital per trade.

Risk Per Trade: Calculate the dollar amount you're comfortable risking based on your risk percentage and account size. This defines the maximum loss you're willing to incur.

Setting Stop-Loss and Take-Profit Levels - Precision in Action

Stop-Loss Orders: Place stop-loss orders at levels that align with your trading strategy and risk tolerance. These levels should be chosen strategically to minimize potential losses.

Take-Profit Orders: Determine take-profit levels based on your risk-reward ratio and the potential price movement of the currency pair. This ensures you lock in profits at a predefined point.

Position Sizing - Balancing Risk and Reward

Position Size Calculation: Calculate the position size for each trade based on your stop-loss distance and the dollar amount you're willing to risk. This ensures consistency in risk across trades.

Lot Sizes: Choose appropriate lot sizes that align with your risk tolerance. Standard lots, mini lots, and micro lots allow you to fine-tune your position size.

Diversification - Spreading the Risk

Currency Pairs: Avoid over-concentration in a single currency pair. Diversify your trades across multiple pairs to spread risk.

Correlation Analysis: Consider the correlation between currency pairs. Negative correlation can offset risk exposure.

Money Management: Maximizing Longevity

Money management encompasses broader strategies that focus on optimizing your overall trading performance and ensuring your trading journey is sustainable over the long term.

Pyramid Strategy - Gradual Scaling

Adding to Winning Positions: In a pyramid strategy, you add to winning positions as the trade moves in your favor. This allows you to capitalize on momentum while managing risk.

Scaling Out: Scale out of positions by gradually closing a portion of the trade as it moves in your favor. This locks in profits while keeping some exposure for potential further gains.

Position Size Adjustments - Adapting to Market Conditions

Volatility-Based Position Sizing: Adjust your position size based on market volatility. In high volatility conditions, reduce position size to manage risk.

Fixed Fractional Position Sizing: Determine your position size as a fraction of your trading capital. As your capital grows or declines, your position size adjusts proportionally.

Risk-Reward Ratios - Balancing Potential and Risk

Favorable Ratios: Seek trades with a risk-reward ratio of 1:2 or better. This means potential profit is at least twice the potential loss.

Assessing Trade Viability: Assess whether a trade's potential profit justifies the potential loss before entering the trade.

Drawdowns and Recovery: Drawdowns are inevitable. Develop a plan to recover from drawdowns and regain profitability.

Risk Reduction in Drawdowns: During drawdowns, consider reducing your risk per trade or temporarily reducing your trading size.

Trading Psychology - The Harmony of Mind and Strategy

Emotional Discipline: Maintain emotional discipline by adhering to your risk management and money management rules. Avoid impulsive decisions driven by fear or greed.

Long-Term Perspective: Focus on the long-term picture rather than short-term wins or losses. Consistency and discipline are the keys to success.

The Symphony of Risk and Money Management

Risk management and money management are the twin guardians of your trading capital. By implementing strategic risk management techniques and optimizing your money management strategies, you fortify your trading foundation and elevate your potential for sustained success in the dynamic forex market.

As we venture further into advanced trading strategies, trading psychology, and real-world applications, remember that your journey as a trader is not solely defined by profits, but by your ability to navigate challenges, adapt to changing conditions, and emerge stronger with each trade.

In the intricate tapestry of forex trading, mastery is attained not only through knowledge but also through the adept application of advanced trading strategies. This chapter transcends the realm of basics, delving into the nuanced techniques that enable traders to navigate the ever-shifting currents of the market with finesse and precision. From scalpels to algorithms, each strategy represents a unique approach to trading, catering to diverse risk tolerances, timeframes, and market conditions.

CHAPTER X

Scalping - Seizing Swift Opportunities

Scalping is the art of swift and nimble trading, capitalizing on micro price movements to generate rapid profits. Traders who embrace this strategy are characterized by their lightning-fast decision-making and the ability to enter and exit trades within minutes or even seconds. Scalping requires intense focus, discipline, and a thorough understanding of market dynamics. This strategy is not for the faint of heart, as it demands split-second decisions and precise execution.

Key Elements of Scalping

Tight Spreads: Scalpers thrive on minimal spreads to minimize transaction costs.

High-Frequency Trading: Scalpers execute numerous trades in a single day, often within minutes or seconds.

M1-M5 Timeframes: Scalping typically occurs on lower timeframes, such as M1 (1-minute) or M5 (5-minute), to capture micro price movements.

Use of Indicators: Scalpers often rely on indicators like moving averages, Bollinger Bands, and oscillators for rapid analysis.

Day Trading: Navigating Intraday Trends

Day trading involves executing trades within a single trading day, capturing short-term trends and market movements. Day traders analyze price charts, technical indicators, and fundamental developments to identify potential opportunities. Unlike scalping, day trading allows for slightly longer holding periods, typically ranging from a few minutes to several hours. Successful day traders possess the ability to adapt swiftly to changing market conditions and manage risk effectively.

Key Strategies for Day Trading

Trend Following: Identify and trade in the direction of the prevailing intraday trend.

Breakout Trading: Trade breakouts of key support or resistance levels on shorter timeframes.

News-Based Trading: Exploit short-term price volatility resulting from news releases or economic events.

Scalping Strategies: Apply scalping techniques for quick profits within the intraday timeframe.

Swing Trading: Riding the Waves of Momentum

Swing trading is a strategy that aims to capture intermediate price movements within a trend. Traders who adopt this approach seek to identify trends that last several days to weeks and ride the price waves within them. Swing traders utilize technical analysis to identify entry and exit points, while also considering fundamental factors that could influence the market. Patience is a key attribute for swing traders, as they wait for trends to unfold before capitalizing on them.

Key Elements of Swing Trading

Technical Analysis: Rely on technical indicators, chart patterns, and trendlines to identify potential swing trade setups.

Market Timing: Enter positions based on the anticipated continuation or reversal of established trends.

Position Sizing: Adjust position size based on the expected duration of the swing trade.

Position Trading: Patience for Long-Term Gains

Position trading is a strategy suited for patient traders who are willing to hold positions for weeks, months, or even years. This approach focuses on capturing long-term trends and larger market movements. Position traders rely on fundamental analysis to identify currency pairs with strong underlying trends and economic fundamentals. They accept that their positions might experience short-term volatility but aim to capitalize on the potential for substantial gains over time.

Strategies for Position Trading

Fundamental Analysis: Base trading decisions on fundamental factors, such as economic indicators and central bank policies.

Diversification: Spread risk across multiple currency pairs to minimize exposure.

Rollover and Carry Trades: Consider interest rate differentials to earn rollover interest and profit from carry trades.

Breakout Trading - Capitalizing on Price Breakouts

Breakout trading involves identifying key support and resistance levels and entering trades when the price breaks out of these levels. Traders seek to capitalize on strong market momentum following a breakout. Conversely, range trading involves identifying periods of consolidation and trading within the established range. Range traders aim to buy at support and sell at resistance until a breakout occurs. Both strategies require a strong understanding of technical analysis and risk management.

Effective Breakout Strategies

Identifying Breakout Points: Monitor consolidation patterns, such as triangles and rectangles, to identify potential breakout points.

Confirmation: Wait for confirmation of a breakout through higher volume or strong price momentum before entering the trade.

False Breakout Management: Be prepared for false breakouts by using stop-loss orders and closely monitoring price action.

Algorithmic Trading (Algo) - The Rise of Machines

Algorithmic trading, often referred to as algo trading or automated trading, leverages computer programs to execute trades based on predefined criteria. Algorithms analyze vast amounts of data, monitor markets in real-time, and execute trades at speeds impossible for humans to achieve. Algo trading strategies range from simple scripts to complex machine learning models. This approach requires a deep understanding of programming, data analysis, and market dynamics.

Advantages of Algorithmic Trading

Speed and Efficiency: Algorithms execute trades at lightning speed, reducing manual errors and optimizing execution.

Emotionless Execution: Algorithms remove emotional biases from trading decisions, ensuring consistency.

Backtesting and Optimization: Algorithms can be backtested and optimized using historical data to refine strategies.

As this chapter concludes, remember that there is no one-size-fits-all approach to trading. Each advanced strategy is a brushstroke on the canvas of your trading journey, allowing you to express your unique style and adapt to various market conditions. Mastery lies not in replicating others' success, but in understanding the nuances of each strategy and tailoring them to fit your risk appetite, trading personality, and goals.

With a diversified arsenal of advanced strategies, you're poised to elevate your trading prowess and embrace the multifaceted world of forex trading with artful precision.

Don't worry about what the markets are going to do, worry about what you are going to do in response to the markets.

MICHAEL CARR

In the labyrinthine world of forex trading, a winning mindset is the elixir that transforms novices into seasoned traders. This chapter is an expedition into the depths of trading psychology, a journey that unravels the intricate tapestry of emotions, cognitive patterns, and behavioral traits that shape every trading decision.

CHAPTER XI

Understanding Trading Psychology - Navigating the Inner Terrain

Beneath the surface of charts and indicators lies the realm of trading psychology — an exploration of the human psyche in the context of the financial markets. It's the subtle dance of emotions, the ceaseless chatter of thoughts, and the instincts that can lead to triumph or downfall.

Managing Emotions: Fear, Greed, Overconfidence

Fear, the apprehension of loss, and greed, the yearning for profit, are powerful emotions that underpin many trading decisions. Navigating them requires a balance between cautiousness and calculated risk-taking. Yet, it's the treacherous terrain of overconfidence that can truly sabotage even the most diligent trader. The battle against these emotions demands introspection, discipline, and strategies for their mastery.

Embracing Losses and Cutting Losses

Embracing losses is akin to acknowledging the inevitability of rain in a stormy sea. Losses are the tuition fees in the school of trading; every loss carries lessons that, if heeded, lead to growth. The art lies in not clinging to losing trades out of desperation but in knowing when to cut losses, thereby preserving your trading capital and emotional well-being.

Cultivating a Winning Mindset

Goal Setting - Paving the Path to Achievement

Goals are the compass that guides your trading journey. They are the lighthouses that beckon you forward even in the midst of market turbulence. Yet, goals must be well-defined, with clear parameters and realistic timelines. They serve as beacons, illuminating the path to success while steering you away from the treacherous waters of impulsive trading.

Positive Self-Talk: Fueling Self-Belief

The power of the spoken word transcends trading. Positive self-talk nurtures self-belief, that invaluable ally that propels you forward when doubt creeps in. It's a conversation with yourself that builds resilience and resilience fosters success. By acknowledging your capabilities and replacing self-limiting thoughts with affirmations, you fortify the mental foundation of a winning trader.

Visualization - Creating Your Future

Visualization is the art of shaping your destiny in the theater of your mind. It's about creating a mental movie of your trading success, rehearsing the scripts of profitable trades, and envisioning yourself making sound decisions with unwavering confidence. Visualization primes your mind to execute your trading strategies flawlessly when the time comes to act.

Maintaining Emotional Balance and Mindfulness

Mindfulness is the bridge between emotion and rationality. It's the art of staying present in the moment, even amidst market turmoil. As you practice mindfulness techniques like meditation and deep breathing, you cultivate the ability to observe your emotions without letting them dictate your decisions. This equilibrium is your anchor in the tempestuous sea of trading.

Detaching from Outcomes and Building Resilience

Market outcomes are as fickle as the wind, often defying even the most sophisticated analyses. Detaching from these outcomes doesn't signify indifference; it's about focusing on the process rather than fixating on profits or losses. Building resilience means recognizing that while you can't control market outcomes, you can control how you respond to them.

Developing Resilience - Bouncing Back from Challenges

Resilience is the art of rebounding from setbacks with renewed vigor. It's about transforming losses into lessons and failures into stepping stones. Developing resilience is akin to forging armor for your trading journey; it equips you with the ability to adapt, learn, and evolve in response to changing market conditions.

Building a Support Network - The Strength of Community

In the solitary realm of trading, a sense of community is a lifeline. Seeking mentorship from experienced traders and participating in trading groups offers insights, guidance, and camaraderie. The collective wisdom of a supportive network bolsters your resolve and provides perspective during challenging times.

As we draw the curtain on this comprehensive guide to mastering the currency markets, a tapestry of knowledge and insight unfurls. From the fundamental concepts to advanced strategies, we have embarked on a journey that equips you with the tools, techniques, and mindset to navigate the ever-shifting currents of forex trading.

We began by laying a solid foundation, understanding the intricacies of forex, selecting the right broker, and setting up your trading environment. We then delved into the heart of analysis — technical and fundamental — unveiling the methods that enable you to decode market patterns and anticipate currency movements.

Building upon these foundations, we explored the art of crafting a trading strategy that aligns with your goals, while safeguarding your capital through robust risk management. Armed with strategies for executing trades, managing positions, and adapting to market events, you gained the capacity to navigate the forex landscape with poise and prudence.

Yet, beyond the mechanics lies the heart of a trader — the psychology that shapes every decision. With an unwavering focus on developing a winning mindset, you learned to manage emotions, cultivate resilience, and detach from outcomes. This mental fortitude, intertwined with your technical acumen, forms the bedrock of trading success.

In a world where technology is reshaping trading paradigms, we explored advanced strategies that harness the power of algorithms and capitalize on diverse market trends. From scalping to algorithmic trading, each strategy is a brushstroke that crafts your unique trading portrait.

As you stand at the crossroads of knowledge and action, remember that trading is a journey, not a destination. The currency markets are both a labyrinth and a canvas — a realm of challenges and opportunities waiting to be explored. Armed with the wisdom gained from this guide, you possess the tools to not only navigate this landscape but to leave your indelible mark upon it.

May your path be guided by disciplined analysis, fearless execution, and a resolute mindset. With each trade, you step further into the realm of possibility, crafting your own narrative amidst the intricate dance of currencies. As you embark on your trading odyssey, remember that success is not a destination — it's a journey, and you are now equipped to traverse it with wisdom, strategy, and the mindset of a triumphant trader.